Resonance of Sentiments

Sherwin Purushothaman

BookLeaf Publishing

India | USA | UK

Presentation by *BookLeaf Publishing*

Web: www.bookleafpub.com

E-mail: info@bookleafpub.com

ISBN:9789360943738

First edition 2024

DEDICATION

In loving memory of two remarkable figures who shaped the early chapters of my journey: my beloved sister, Prerna, and my cherished grandmother, Saraswathy. Though they are no longer with us, I am certain they would have beamed with pride to witness my transformation into a published author. Their unwavering support and enduring love continue to inspire me every day.

ACKNOWLEDGEMENT

I extend my deepest gratitude to those who have supported me on this creative odyssey – friends, family, and readers alike. Your encouragement fuels my passion for poetry, inspiring me to continue exploring the boundless terrain of human expression.

PREFACE

In the realm of poetry, words are the brushstrokes of the soul, painting vivid portraits of the human experience. *Resonance of Sentiments* is a collection that delves into the intimate mosaic of life, weaving together the kaleidoscope of emotions that define our existence. Each poem is a window into my perception, a reflection of the world as I see it, coloured by my experiences, thoughts, and emotions.

For those familiar with my previous works, *Shadows of my Imaginations* and *Inklings of Bonds and Emotions*, this collection marks a continuation of my poetic journey. Just as shadows dance across the canvas of our minds and bonds tether us to the hearts of others, these poems seek to capture the essence of the human condition in all its complexity.

As with any work of art, interpretation is subjective. These poems invite you to embark on a journey of introspection, to explore the depths of your own heart and mind. May you find resonance in these verses, and may they serve as companions on your own voyage of self-discovery.

So, dear reader, I invite you to immerse yourself in the pages of *Resonance of Sentiments*. May these poems stir something within you, igniting a spark of connection that transcends the written word.

With heartfelt sincerity,
Sherwin Purushothaman

Table of Contents

A Tale of Chance

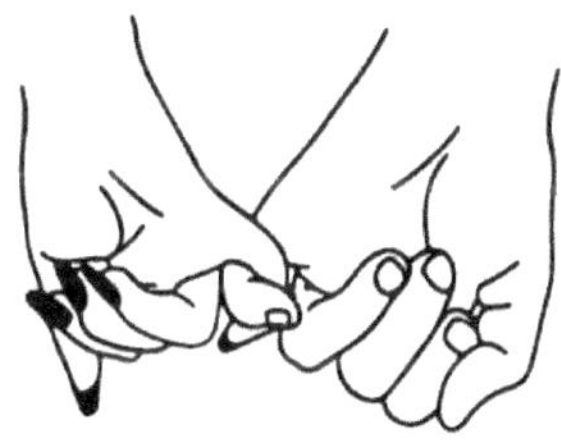

In echoes of trains, arrivals and goodbyes,
I stand on the platform, anticipation in my eyes.
Contrary to my nerves uncertain of a hopeful
flair,
She emerged from the arriving train, a breath of
fresh air.

She alighted from the train, a vision so bright,
In a salwar kameez, colors taking flight
I held compliments back, a cautious refrain,
Fear of flirtation, in my heart's domain.

Her lips adorned with vibrant hues,
Her confidence blooms with every muse.
Her smile, a canvas of secrets untold,
Dimples whisper stories, a beauty to behold.

Accessories adorned, a perfect blend,
Matching her dress, a style to commend.
Less often do you meet a woman so rare,
Grace and resilience, her aura declare

In a moment of equations gone astray,
She, a goddess, and I, a lad, in dismay.
Pressure mounts, sweat flows with every
thought,
A water bottle in hand, my thirst it sought.

Etiquette in play, water I offered her with grace,
She hesitated, then sipped, a subtle embrace.
Gulped down the last drop, with a gaze so fine,
I smiled, "how sweet is the water," a moment
divine.

Little did I know, a wizard's spell would get cast,
An accidental phrase shall lead to a connection
so vast.
Deeply bound by this sweet misunderstanding,
A memory grew to cherish, a valentine
everlasting.

The Lone Voyager

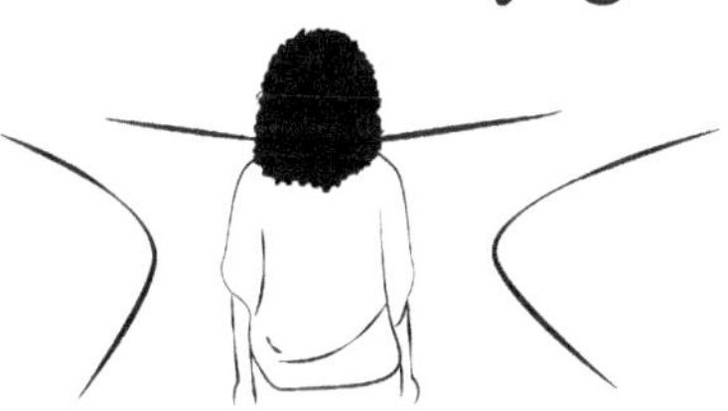

Amidst the whispers of the world, she stands,
her mind ponders in a labyrinth of dreams.
Lost in the music of her own silent bands,
where echoes of wonder flow in silent streams.

In contemplative grace, her mind takes flight,
Thoughts swirling like stars in the deep of the
night.
Each idea is a universe, every notion a plot,
A girl who dwells where musings tie the knot.

Each soul is a canvas, deemed in a cast,
her verdicts are swift, stereotypes steadfast.
Shadows' sights land her in despair's embrace,
convinced she is that every gaze holds no tender
grace.

A wanderer of solo trips, embracing the breeze,
when constellations guide, her heart finds ease,
Amidst each sunrise, she's found her own throne,
A lone voyager, in lands yet unknown.

Digital Love

In a weary day's fatigue, my spirits low,
Seeking solace, a decision to bestow.
To find reprieve in the virtual domain,
Online, the remedy to alleviate the strain.

Connected to the web, the setup began,
Bytes in motion, a techno-woven plan.
Craving for content, a browsing spree,
In the dance of data, a modern jubilee.

Messenger activated, you, my online mate,
Love in bits, a connection to contemplate.
A chat unfolded, texts weaving a tale,
A steady start, a digital trail.

Your bitmap face, in the virtual frame,
A pixelated enchantment, love's new name.
In this coded landscape, an error-free vow,
Linked together, our digital love shall plough.

I'll scan for viruses, clear the path,
In our digital love, I'll do the math.
In this binary life, our hearts aligned,
A love story, in the digital bind.

Sarcastic Melody

In her supercilious gaze, I am always left
oblivious,
All my perfect gestures reduced to a paltry
effort.
A self-made esteem, a mind poignant and bold,
But with this lass, caution's story told

Not lacking in pride or strength, you see,
Chauvinist and egoist, that's me.
In the depths of her sarcasm, I still find allure,
A question lingers, why do I endure?

Her dry wit cuts through, a sharp blade,
A cautionary tale of a friendship betrayed.
Yet, a fascination, a pull so strong,
Her essence whispers, a melody's song.

In her, lies beauty, not just in form,
But in conscience clear, through life's storm.
Though her ways may vex, challenge the norm,
In her enticement, I find my heart warm.

Theater of Life

In the theater of life, we take the stage,
A formal responsibility, our role to engage.
With every step, we showcase what we know,
Striving with all we have, putting on a show.

Responsibilities loom, not to be slighted,
A serious reality, never to be blighted.
Unlimited tasks, a relentless stream,
No pay, no pity, just a distant dream.

Duties call, our presumed obligation,
Undeniable, without reservation.
Efforts expended, for quality's sake,
Yet appreciation, we often forsake.

Like premiums paid, to secure our life,
Parents' sacrifices, through joy and strife.
Their investment, our guiding light,
Their love, our anchor in the night.

Sacrifices made, dreams put on hold,
Their hopes and dreams, ours to uphold.
For in their eyes, we're meant to shine,
An unwavering, responsible line.

So let us embrace our roles with grace,
And in fulfilling duties, find our place.
For in this journey, we'll surely find,
The essence of life, in love intertwined.

Your Animosity

Survived an accusing cult
A day to remember on a night of insult,
The pain was slow yet it hurt,
A cleansed soul yet a prey of your dirt.

Efforts to mend ways are now in vain,
as you blindly ride on the path of mistrust.
Hatred reeks out of your thoughts insane,
Your vision impaired, all you see is dust.

Delusion in minds cannot kill legacy.
Darkness is only a matter of time.
Apology cannot make the dead, alive
Redemption doesn't hide a crime.

The hammer of negativity hurled in protest,
has put my walls of reputation to the test.
Lesson learnt; but now it's time for payback.
In your world of anarchy, I'll instill the respect
you lack.

The Rat Race

The world today is in a relentless rat race,
takes up all your grit to survive at this pace.
Mists of modesty are now polluted with selfish
desires.
All that everyone wants is to salvage empires.

Blank canvases thrive to be painted in victory.
Debt and slavery are chosen over being free.
In this race for fortune, fame, and more,
We forget to cherish the moments we adore.

There is no empathy for the weary.
Through all the tantrums, you still need to keep
yourself steady.
Stress doesn't reduce even when you're sick.
Every morning, you ought to prepare yourself to
face the music.

So lift your morale up, especially after you go
down in flames.
Master your strokes to play and win those
diplomatic games.
Though the highs and lows of destiny are true by
design,
You'll learn to slog through, come rain or shine.

The Job Hunt

In the hunt for employment, I embarked,
Cashing in on prospects, hope not marred
Yet, denial met me at every turn,
Baseless excuses, reasons to spurn.

Restless, I sought leads from all around,
Friends, foes, relatives, none were found.
Respect waned, morale bruised, bleeding sore,
Betrayed by fate, God's games, what's in store?

A friend's doubt pierced, my confidence it
shook,
Deemed me inferior like a closed book.
Questions arose, the end in sight,
Happy endings, mere fiction, not right.

Hard work's worth, against luck's cruel jest,
Bravery tested, yet fate's unrest.
Law of Attraction, a tale askew,
Exception to norms, destiny's view.

Ceteris paribus, assumptions fail,
My path diverges, beyond the veil.
My job hunt continues to be strong, though
results delay,
Hope persists, in the face of dismay.

Work from Home Dilemma

Waking up to alarms, rushing through the
chores,
Boarding the crowded trains that reek of sweat
and loud snores.
Racing against time, which continues to play
mean,
Going to the office daily had become routine.

Perspiring profusely, I managed to reach my
workstation,
which cried of never-ending work and unread
emails.
After dealing with the work pressures, I
commuted back home
with a tired mind and a body demanding
vacation.

Then came the coronavirus which spread into a
pandemic,
All interactions became online; be it official or
academic.
With commuting to office banned in this
situation so bad,
I felt I'd save a lot of time which I never had.

Lousy canteen food was soon to change to
healthy homemade food.
Work from home also promised family bonding
to be good,
Presenting a chance to get back with friends who
were off touch.
Most importantly, I would get the de-stress
which I craved for so much.

As I lay on bed, relaxing my bones,
enjoying the seasons of "Game of Thrones".
The Government, all of a sudden, announced the
lockdown,
citing reasons of increasing infected cases in
town

With the lockdown imposed, reality showed a
different side.
Working beyond office hours surprisingly
became implied.
Responsibilities of cleaning, washing and
cooking couldn't be kept aside,
resulting in silly fights with close ones and my
sleep deprived.

Now I hope for things to be functional and
regular again,
So that I can get back to my lifestyle of a snob.
I miss my workstation, my colleagues and my
routine.
And given the challenges at home, I miss my
desk job.

The Pandemic Survival

The world today, dreads a dangerous virus
Incurable, it poses a health threat to all of us.
While some stayed safe in the confines of their
home,
The choice-less continued to travel and roam.

Forced to move beyond the shielded trajectory,
Left alone to battle in the absence of cure.
Despite the valor at this bio war, sweet ain't
victory.
Good health is what they failed to endure.

Sad to see lives succumb to this pandemic,
a reason good enough for everyone to panic.
But sorry has been the state of those who
survived,
as they were stigmatized and remained
help-deprived.

This discrimination demotivates the mind,
makes one feel like an untouchable kind.
Forged out of immunity, though armors were built,
the cold shoulders treat them to lead a life of guilt.

While self-protection is the advisory nationwide,
Avoiding pandemic survivors ain't justified.
Having walked the dark alleys of their illness episode,
All they seek is a light of hope at the end of the road.

Tsunami

Pleasant was the day as people relaxed on the
beach,
unaware of the shock they were about to get,
The levels of normalcy were about to breach,
Unseen and unheard would be the nature of this
threat.

It came unexpectedly and without a warning.
Striking everything that came in its path,
Properties were destroyed and humans left
mourning,
such was the rage of nature unleashing its wrath.

Displaced children kept begging for food,
their bodies were bruised and not looking so
good.
The rich and the poor were both slayed.
Unbiased by culture, now everyone prayed.

In an instant, tragedy struck with relentless
force,
Leaving those impacted bewildered, without
remorse.
Rising tides surged from the ocean's profound,
Swiftly engulfing, what we now term a tsunami's
sound.

Life – A Rollercoaster ride

Life's a ride, a rollercoaster's sway,
Climbing high, then swiftly, it takes you away.
A choice to ride or step aside,
Destiny's coaster, an inescapable guide.

Confidence and pride slowly fade,
As sufferings deepen in destiny's shade.
Revival seems a distant plea,
Worst scenarios surround, a harsh decree

Ethics shift, prayers rise,
Luck elusive, happiness denies
Luck's pursuit, a relentless chase,
Foolproof attempts meet an unjust embrace.

Logic lost in wonderland,
Attempts foiled by an unseen hand.
Allies fade, or masks they wear,
Losing battles, everywhere.

Know your weaknesses, in the tide you flowed,
Challenged not in speed, but against it you
strode.
Trust your instincts, patience is your shield,
Inner determination is the weapon to wield.

No one knows you more than yourself,
Against unsolicited advice, stand firm, stay true
to oneself.
Aberrant times, a passing phase,
Blend abilities, feelings, navigate life's maze.

Paradigm Shift

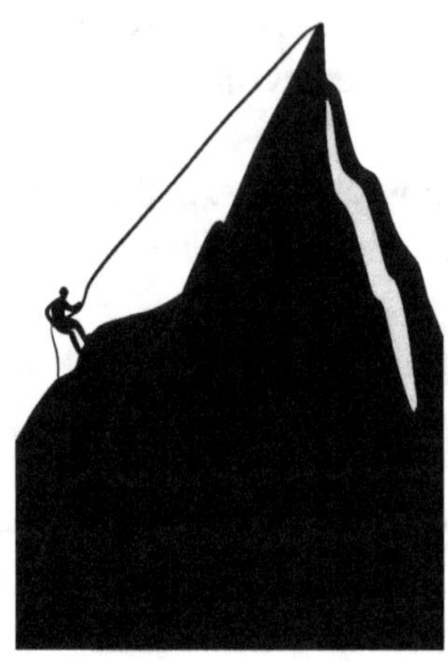

In stringent times, facing life's snags,
I learned to smile, defeating their hoods' drags.
This little part, my Happiness named,
Through challenges, a resilient flame.

To value relationships, it took some time,
Amid family, friends, in this dream, I climb.
Once laid-back, self-caring, now grown,
An incandescent personality, proudly shown.

Calculative, meticulous, my past demeanor,
Limited friendships, an outcome not leaner.
Fate's twist ameliorated my chauvinist stance,
Thanks to my sister, a friendship's advance.

She set a paradigm, an ideal friend,
Accessible, caring, on her, they depend.
Lesson learned, no point in strife,
Value loved ones, the essence of life.

Humans enact emotions, a varied display,
Be reasonable with others, let kindness sway.
Unreasonable with oneself, a key to success,
Hunger for more, embrace self-progress.

Critics

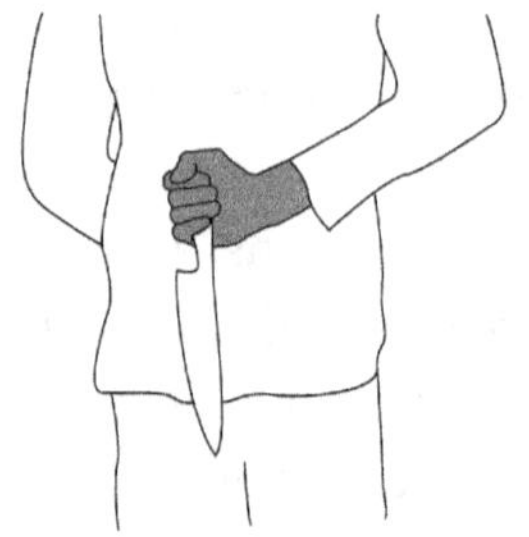

With harsh gaze, critics paint flaws bright,
Salt wounds with scorn, ignite our plight.
But hold, dear friend, before you curse,
A hidden truth, unfolds in verse

Imagine you, a grad so grand,
Jobless, waiting, hand in hand.
Your father speaks, a pointed barb,
"The race is fierce, don't lose your guard."

Hate him not, he stirs the fire,
Ignites your light, fuels your desire.
They see your strength, though shadows fall,
Motivators, disguised, they brawl.

Critics guide, in the cloak of the foe,
While flatterers whisper, let them go.
Their harshness, a twisted grace,
Unveils the truth, in your own space

So next they strike, with words unkind,
Remember well, the strength you'll find.
For even thorns, though sharp and cold,
Can forge a future, brave and bold.

Anger's Fire

In silent rage, a fire burns,
Unseen, unheard, a lesson spurns.
It festers deep, a brewing storm,
While reason's voice is left forlorn.

The ego swells, a twisted pride,
Convinced of right, with logic tied.
Each misstep magnifies the wrong,
As sanity is cast along.

The body numb, a puppet frail,
Obeys no will, begins to fail.
It wanders lost, in actions strange,
A hollow shell, consumed by change.

The urge to scream, to lash out, to break,
But silence reigns, a deadly ache.
Within the flames, a lonely plea,
"Who cares what others think of me?"

But ashes only fill the void,
When anger's fire has been destroyed.
The world moves on, oblivious to the plight,
Leaving the aftermath of a silent night.

Lost friends and trust, a bitter taste,
A hollowness that cannot be erased.
The cost of pride, a heavy toll,
For lessons learned, a lonely soul.

The victor's crown, a crown of thorns,
A silent war, with battles borne.
Was this the victory you sought?
A heavy price, dearly bought.

Jealousy of Self Pride

In the realm where jealousy reigns,
A throne of insecurity it maintains.
Losing supremacy to those deemed better,
It sparks envy, a consuming fetter.

Competing fiercely to increase one's sway,
In a ceaseless pursuit, day by day.
But beneath this envy, a thin divide,
Pride and jealousy, from the same wellspring
derived.

Jealousy, a broadcast of frustration's glare,
With whispers of defaming rivals to repair.
A cold war stance in this proxy fight,
As integrity fades in envy's blight.

Yet pride, a beacon of self-respect's glow,
Untarnished by peers' performance, it does
show.
An accomplishment's display, not boastful
veneer,
Above the fray, without fear.

Some may decry pride as a negative force,
But in its rightful place, it charts a steady course.
Not a hyperbolic show, but a stance refined,
Maintaining innocence, character aligned.

So let jealousy fade, a response to compare,
And let pride, from within, a reactive air.
For in this balance, authenticity thrives,
Where jealousy wanes, and true pride survives.

The Gift of Ignorance

Mockers roam, a soulless breed,
Barbs they fling, plant doubt's dark seed.
A perfect day, in tatters torn,
Confidence shaken, spirit worn.

Why twist the knife in another's plight?
Can't joy exist bathed in pure light?
Live in your lane, let others roam,
Happiness thrives not built on home

Destroyed by spite, but hold on tight,
If strong you won't stand, their words take flight
The sting may linger, a fleeting pain,
But those who matter, love won't wane.

Their power wanes when met with grace,
A silent strength, a winning race.
Ignore their taunts, let pity bloom,
Fools trip and fall while flowers bloom.

"Don't let them dim your inner spark",
Whisper this truth within the dark.
Let goals achieved be your reply,
Soar high above where shadows lie.

For angels fear not fools' clumsy dance,
They twirl in whispers, given a chance.
With purpose rise, with dreams take flight,
And prove their mockery, a fading light.

The Rise of the Fallen

Beneath the blazing sun's relentless gaze,
The hot afternoon unfolds in a fiery haze.
Sweat beads form, as the heat's clutch tightens,
Nature's warmth and beauty, in this moment,
enlightens.

In the scorching sun, it tried to fly so high,
A dehydrated kite, against the sky.
Its paper wings, once vibrant and bright,
Now brittle and dry, a spectral sight.

Amidst the skies so wide, where the eyes can
barely see,
a falling bird, its wings failing to open free,
fainting on concrete, losing its gentle grace,
reminding us of life's fleeting, fragile embrace.

Rescued from the heat, its trembling chest.
Picked up by gentle hands, this tired bird found
rest.
With tender care, it was nursed back to life.
Now, in the sky, it soars, free from strife.

In shadows deep, we've often thought to hide
Given up on dreams that once did bide.
But still, a spark within us softly glows.
A whisper of hope, a chance to grow.

From fallen depths, we find our strength.
In trials faced, we go to any length.
With every stumble, we learn to prize,
the power within, to once more rise.

A Story of Sacrifice

In the quiet of night, burdened shoulders stoop,
His journey continues in a winding, uphill loop.
Silent struggles etched upon lines worn,
His sacrifices describe a story quietly borne.

In the crossfire of words, a lone figure stands,
Echoes of criticism, like relentless sands.
Every step dissected, every flaw laid bare,
Yet resilience blooms, amidst the critical air.

From growing up admiring the beauty of life
to finding himself on the edge of a knife,
dealing with knots of problems which can't be
opened with ease,
A man maturely journeys through life
slowly untangling from burdens in his quest to
embrace peace.

Through deserts of doubt, every man seeks the divine,
as he searches for answers about his present design.
His battles have not always ended in glory,
yet he gets up to fight, just to finish his story.

A father's birthday wish

As your tiny fingers grasped my trembling hand,
I felt eternal bliss in this life's grand strand.
In awe, my heart swelled with joy,
when your birth was announced, my boy.

As you grew older, your speech now clear,
You played and danced, devoid of fear.
With each step forward, you embraced the sun,
That's my boy, a tale yet to be spun.

A father's love, a bond that I can't erase,
always guiding you through life's unknown
chase,
Though time may fly and seasons swiftly pass,
My love for you, my son, will eternally amass.

May each dawn greet you with joy's sweet
embrace,
As life unfolds, may love be your grace.
On this special day, as candles softly alight,
Happy birthday, dear son, may your future be
bright.

Granny's Love

The best babysitters, in truth, they stand,
Guiding with care, a gentle hand.
She puts us to sleep with stories untold,
And chases away tears, brave and bold.

Terrible deeds melt in a twinkling glance,
Replaced by wonder, a sweet, joyful dance.
Not mother, though her love's immense,
But grandma's heart, a finer essence.

Her hands that work, they never tire,
A tireless spirit, burning fire.
No anger flares, her smile's a sun,
Warmth for all, a race well-run.

From earth to the moon, they'd move in a blink,
A love so fierce, it makes the soul think.
No sweeter refuge, no cozier nest,
than grandma's warm heart, a haven of rest.

Forever and always, a bond that holds tight,
Through darkness and sunshine, a guiding light.
When the world seems cold, a hand to hold true,
A grandmother's love, forever for you.

Teachers

In the nurturing embrace of home,
A mother's love, steadfast and true,
Yet in the classroom, seeds are sown,
Teachers, like mothers, guide us through.

With patience, they impart each morsel,
Linking lessons to life's grand scheme,
Guiding us through every portal,
Treating us like a cherished dream.

From history's vast tapestry, they weave,
Revealing how civilizations evolved,
In geometry's angles, we perceive,
The shapes of knowledge they resolved.

They are the founts of wisdom's flow,
Guiding us through learning's maze,
Instilling values, high and low,
Guiding us through life's vast ways.

Like gems unearthed from deep within,
Knowledge they bestow with care,
For us, they tirelessly begin,
To nurture minds beyond compare

Dear teachers, pillars of our days,
Without whom we'd wander aimlessly
Though sometimes feared, in myriad ways,
They sculpt us into who we'll be.

Indian Spirit

In the heart of a country, where dreams aspire,
A republic's flame burns like a fervent fire.
'Unity in diversity' has been a timeless theme.
Threads of culture weave a vibrant Indian
dream.

From Himalayan peaks to the Ganges wide,
A nation's spirit can be seen in every stride.
Indian constitution is a guiding tide,
Justice and liberty, side by side.

Majestic symbols like the Ashoka's wheel,
A pledge to truth symbolizes the common seal.
Democracy's dance, a lively reel,
In every heart is the nation's zeal.

A Republic's dawn, a new birthright,
Freedom's anthem, a soaring flight.
In laws and rights, a beacon bright,
India's republic, a radiant light.

From ancient texts to modern gaze,
Indian spirit, in time's embrace.
Resilient, strong, and ever bright,
A kaleidoscope of pure delight.

India Rising

A rising economic might, a surging tide,
Digital prowess, far and wide.
Science and wisdom, hand in hand,
A nation reborn, for a future unplanned.

From icy peaks to desert's scorching sand,
India's soldiers, a resolute band.
From fertile fields to factories grand,
A youthful workforce, taking a stand.

Global voice, for the voiceless it speaks,
A champion of justice, for the downtrodden it
seeks.
Renewable giants, reaching for the sun,
A fight for clean air, a battle well-won.

Not just on Earth's ground does its prowess
reside,
India's gaze to the heavens, a soaring pride.
Mangalyaan's triumph and a lunar embrace,
Frugal minds and boundless might, a future
space race.

Sports ignite, a fiery display,
Talents unleashed, lighting the way.
Olympic rings and Asian fire,
India's stars soared ever higher.

Challenges remain, a path to be trod,
But the spirit of India, answers to its God.
With unity strong, and purpose so bright,
India's rising, a glorious sight.

Trees

In the embrace of sunlight, sustenance forms,
Nature's brilliance, the ultimate norms.
Dependent on elements, freely gained,
A utilitarian marvel, the tree, so ingrained.

Bestowing gifts for our well-being's sake,
Yet, ingratitude blossoms in a harsh rake.
For major needs, we wield the blade,
But seeds planted ensure the debt's repaid

Diverse in types, nature's grand array,
Each serving a purpose, day by day.
Medicinal wonders, some trees unfold,
A clarion call to plant, a story to be told.

Companions are they, steadfast and true,
Sharing generously, lending without due.
Never seeking payment, fruits bestowed free,
A testament to the importance: plant a tree.

Hawkers

From fragrant spices to fabrics rare,
their stalls offer items beyond compare.
Their voices carry through the urban sprawl,
Hawkers with their skills, captivates us all.

Occupying the footpaths, we'll find these
informal sellers of goods.
The unorganized sector, as the bureaucrats call
them.
Vending everything from fruits to vegetables,
stationeries to flowers;
while fighting their will against the customers'
bargaining powers.

These make-shifters are always armed with
essential accessories.
A humble cart, a weighing scale to measure their
groceries,
just about enough money to tender change to
their customers
and an umbrella to protect them from rains and
the hot summers.

Dealing with the routine banter,
facing buyers, either pleasant or fuming with
anger,
These tricksters know to keep their customers
spellbound,
by enchanting them with freebies and discounts.

Through sun and rain, they persevere,
Their spirits resilient, year after year
In their humble trade, they find their grace,
Hawkers, the heartbeat of the marketplace.

So let us cherish these vendors bold,
Whose stories, often left untold.
In the city's pulse, they find their way,
Hawkers, we salute you every day.

The Trendy Girl

In search of the trendy girl's grace,
Learn her likes, know her taste.
Treat her as a precious pearl,
For she is the gem in your world.

Gift her luxury, lavish and grand,
In her eyes, it's where love stands.
Yet, her loyalty swiftly shifts,
To those with pockets full of gifts.

She craves the thrill of movies and rides,
Shopping sprees where joy abides.
She stands by you through thick and thin,
But beware, when wealth wears thin.

If you provide all she desires,
Your bond will flourish, reaching higher.
But when finances cease to thrive,
Her presence, alas, takes its dive.

Studies

In the realm of learning, we confront certain
truths,
Facts and figures enclose our youths.
History, Civics, Maths, and Science bright,
Together they form our academic plight.

Some find joy in these branches of thought,
Intelligence and knowledge, adorned with
wisdom sought.
They relish the challenge, the studious kind,
Their collars raised with their minds refined.

Yet others find studying a bore,
Pressed to learn, their spirits sore.
Bound by parental will and school fees' weight,
They tread the path, resigned to fate.

Grammar's maze, a daunting climb,
History's tales, a race against time.
Subjects, a burden on tender minds,
Yet, they sculpt and shape the soul's finds.

Studies seem like a cumbersome weight,
For students whose senses struggle to elate.
Yet within these tomes, a power resides
To shape minds anew, where potential abides.

The Idiot Box

In every home, its presence looms,
Casting its glow in dimly lit rooms.
The Idiot Box, a modern-day vice,
Captivating minds with its enticing guise.

With flickering images, it draws us near,
Whispering promises of entertainment sheer.
But behind its screen of radiant light,
Lurks a world of illusion, hidden from sight.

It captivates eyes with tales untold,
Yet often leaves hearts empty and cold.
With its tales of love, drama, and crime,
It weaves a web, stealing away time.

But amidst the chaos, there's wisdom to glean,
If we dare to look beyond the screen.
For within its grasp, lies knowledge profound,
Waiting to be discovered, if we're bound.

So let's not be fooled by its flashy allure,
But instead, seek truth that's pure.
For the Idiot Box, though it may deceive,
Holds within it the power to inspire and relieve.

My Lost Slipper

Not just footwear for my tread,
But a throne for happy tread.
From a shop with a name of renown,
My favorite slipper, soft and brown.

Oh, the joy when I first brought it home,
Now a void where it used to roam.
Slippers I have, a shelf full, and more,
But none with a charm I adored before.

A treasure it was, a comfort so true,
Like a monarch's crown, a loyal, warm hue.
Summer or winter, it never complained,
A featherweight friend, my worries it drained

Envy it drew from those around,
Now lost, my heart with sorrow bound
In my mind, its absence etched clear,
Praying for its return, my hope sincere

So, I mourn the loss of my dear slipper,
Praying it returns, a cherished giver.
For in its simple form, a tale does lie,
Of comfort, joy, and a longing sigh.

www.ingramcontent.com/pod-product-compliance
Lightning Source LLC
La Vergne TN
LVHW021229200726
843509LV00012B/1459

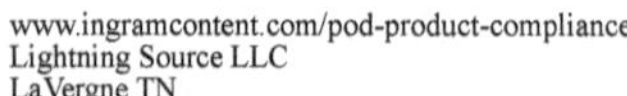